Seasonal Crafts

Winter

Gillian • Chapman

WAYLAND

Seasonal Crafts

Spring • Summer • Autumn • Winter

Series editor: Sarah Doughty
Design and artwork by Gillian Chapman
DTP design by Joyce Chester

First published in 1997 by Wayland Publishers Ltd
61 Western Road, Hove, East Sussex, BN3 1JD

British Library Cataloguing in Publication Data
Chapman, Gillian
   Winter. (Seasonal crafts)
   1. Holiday decorations – Juvenile literature 2. Handicraft –
Juvenile literature
   I. Title
   745.5'941

ISBN 0 7502 1838 X

Printed and bound by G. Canale & C.S.p.A., Borgaro Tse,
Turin

Picture acknowledgements:

B & C Alexander 22; Circa 20 (John Smith); E.T. Archive 10,
24; the Hutchison Library 16; Photri 6, 8; Robert Harding
(Ching Mai) 28; Tony Stone Worldwide 4 (Stephen Studd),
18 (Robert Shafter), 26 (David Young Wolff); Zefa 12.

All commissioned photography, including the cover pictures
by Chris Fairclough. Props made by Gillian Chapman.

Contents

Words that are shown in **bold** are explained in the glossary on page 31.

Winter Time

△ *People enjoy playing in the snow. In this London park they are tobogganing down the icy slopes.*

In many countries, winter can be a very cold time of year. People wrap themselves up in layers of clothes to keep warm. Some animals and plants spend the season resting as a way of escaping from the cold snow and frost when the ground is frozen and there is little food to eat.

Candles and bonfires are an important part of winter. In the past, lighting fires and candles were the only ways to have light and warmth. In winter festivals, the flames of fire are **symbolic**. They show the power that light has over darkness and evil spirits.

Winter Projects

Winter Festivities

Christmas and New Year festivals are times of great celebration all over the world. People decorate their homes, have parties and exchange presents and cards.

Recycling Christmas

After Christmas is over, all the wrapping papers, greetings cards and empty present boxes are usually thrown out. But they could all be recycled and used again. Some of the projects in this book will show you how.

Old cards and gift wrap will all come in useful to make gift boxes, cards and decorations for next Christmas. Start to make a collection now.

Paints and Glues

Poster and powder paints are ideal for most projects. A selection of different sized paint brushes is useful, but also use felt pens for fine detail.

Keep old brushes separate for gluing. PVA glue will stick thick card together. Mix it with water to make papier mâché. Use a glue stick for paper and thin card.

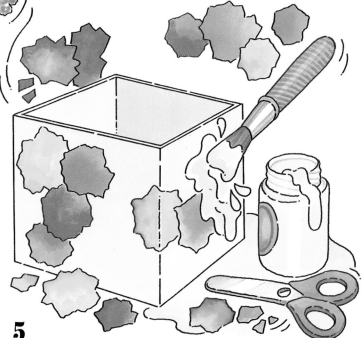

Thanksgiving

Thanksgiving is held on the fourth Thursday in November. It is the day when American families enjoy roast turkey and pumpkin pie and remember their **ancestors** that sailed over from Europe in December 1620.

When the settlers arrived, it was too cold to plant seeds. Many settlers died, but others were helped through the harsh winter by the **native** American Indians. In the spring they planted crops. They held the first Thanksgiving Feast in 1621 to celebrate a good harvest and say thank you to the Indians.

An American family sit around the table together to enjoy a traditional Thanksgiving meal. ▽

Making a Pop-up Turkey Card

You will need:
* Rectangle of thin card
* Scissors
* Pencil and ruler
* Thin card scraps
* Coloured paper scraps
* Glue stick

1 Fold the rectangle of card in half. Cut a strip of card 2 cm wide and half the length of the card. ▽

2 Fold the strip of card in half. Fold back each end by 1 cm. ▽

3 Lay the strip across the centre of the card lining up the centre folds. Glue the strip to the card. △

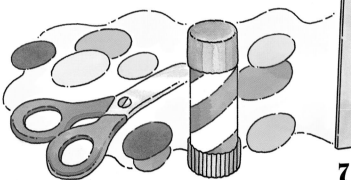

4 Cut out a circle of card, fold it in half and glue it to the strip making sure the folds line up. ▽

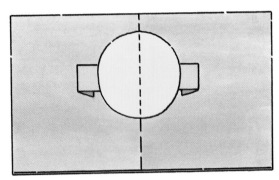

5 Decorate the card by gluing on shapes cut from coloured paper. ▽

7

Advent

Advent is the time leading up to Christmas. The name means 'the coming'. It is when Christians prepare to celebrate the birth of Jesus Christ.

In Europe and America Advent is celebrated with candles and wreaths decorating homes and churches. The wreath has four candles and one is lit for each Sunday in Advent. Advent calendars are very popular to count down the days before Christmas begins.

This child is lighting the candles on the Advent wreath in her church. ▽

Making an Advent Cascade

1 Put one of the sweets into each of the small boxes. Wrap them up securely in the gift wrap. ▽

You will need:
* 24 small boxes
* 24 wrapped sweets
* Christmas gift wrap, ribbon and tinsel
* Scissors
* Sticky tape
* Labels and pen
* Wire coat-hanger

2 Tie each box with the ribbon and label them, marking each with a number 1 to 24. Tie a length of ribbon to each box and attach it to the coat hanger. ▽

4 Cover the wire coat-hanger with extra ribbon or tinsel. Decorate it with any spare decorations. Hang up the Advent Cascade and open a box on each day of Advent. ▽

3 Tie all the boxes to the coat hanger letting them hang at different lengths. ▷

9

St. Nicholas' Day

This portrait of St. Nicholas shows him as a kind old man with a grey curly beard, and was painted hundreds of years after his death. ▷

This is the feast day of St. Nicholas, who died on the 6 December in AD 326. He was a Turkish **bishop**, who is remembered for being kind and generous to children.

Stories tell us that St. Nicholas used to leave small presents in children's shoes. In many northern European countries people give presents on this day. In Amsterdam, in the Netherlands, there is a parade and 'St. Nicholas' rides into the city on a white horse, led by his servant Black Peter.

Making St. Nicholas' Slippers

1 To make a slipper template, draw an oval shape on to a piece of scrap card and cut it out. ▽

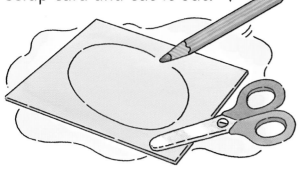

2 Use the card template to make the felt shapes. Place the template on the felt. Draw around it three times and cut out the felt oval shapes. ▽

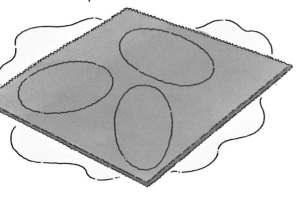

3 Cut one of the felt ovals in half and pin it on top of another. Then neatly sew them together. ▽

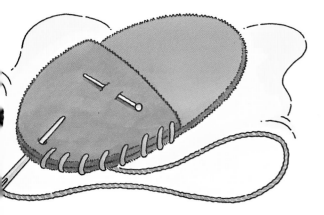

4 Glue felt shapes on to the toe with small dabs of PVA glue. ▽

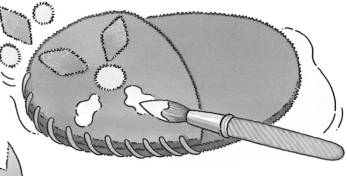

5 Make a small hole in the slipper and thread the ribbon through. Make the second slipper in the same way. Fill them with sweets and hang them on the tree. ▽

Hanukkah

△ *During Hanukkah a small servant candle is used to light one candle each night on the hanukia, until the other eight are alight.*

This is the Jewish Festival of Lights which lasts for eight days in December. Over 2,000 years ago a small Jewish army defeated the **Syrian** army in battle. The Jews returned to their temple to find only one lamp of holy oil left. But by a **miracle** of God, the flame burnt for eight days until more oil could be found.

At Hanukkah Jews remember this miracle by lighting a candle on the **hanukia**. There is one candle for each day of the festival. Families also celebrate by exchanging cards and gifts.

Making a Hanukkah Card

The six-pointed star of David is an important Jewish symbol. This card uses the star as part of the design.

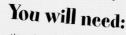
1 To make a six-pointed star, first draw a circle on the paper with a pair of compasses. ▽

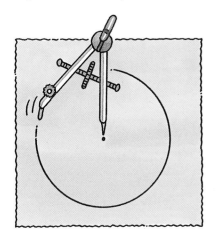 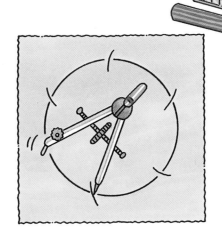 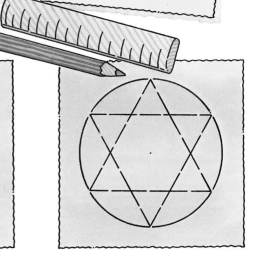

2 Use the compasses to divide the circle **circumference** into six equal parts. △

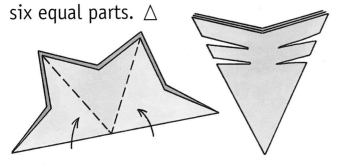

3 Connect the points to form a star. Then cut it out. △

4 Fold the star in half, and then in thirds. Carefully cut small slits in each side. Open up the star and fold back the slits. △

5 Fold a rectangle of card in half and glue the star to the front. ▷

13

Christmas Decorations

In the weeks before Christmas people prepare for the festival by decorating their homes. Here are some ideas to make decorations from scraps of Christmas ribbons, gift wrap and sweet papers.

Making Festive Chains

1 Use scraps of Christmas ribbons of different colours and patterns and cut them into 15 cm lengths. ▷

2 Curl the first length of ribbon and either staple it or glue it together. Attach more lengths to make a chain. ▷

Making Christmas Lanterns

1 Flatten a scrap of gift wrap face down on the table. Glue a sheet of A4 paper to it. When the glue has dried, trim off the surplus gift wrap. ▷

2 Fold the gift wrap in half and make a series of cuts along the length. Then glue the sides together and staple a handle to the top. ▷

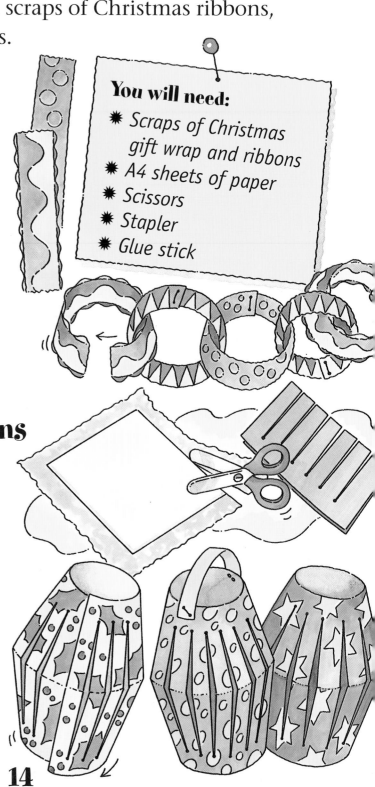

You will need:
* Scraps of Christmas gift wrap and ribbons
* A4 sheets of paper
* Scissors
* Stapler
* Glue stick

Making Dancing Animals

You will need:
* Piece of dark card
* Light coloured pencil
* Scissors
* Hole punch
* Glue stick
* Clear, colourful sweet wrappers
* Christmas ribbon

1 Draw a simple animal shape on dark card with a light pencil. Then cut it out. △

2 Cut shapes out of the animal, with scissors or a hole punch. △

3 Turn the animal over and carefully stick pieces of coloured sweet wrappers over the holes, using small dabs of glue. △

4 Cut out extra details, like antlers, and glue them in place. Attach the ribbon and hang the dancing animal in the window or on the Christmas tree. ▽

Mexican Christmas

In Mexico many kinds of colourful Christmas decorations are made from clay and brightly painted. These are sold in markets during the weeks before Christmas. Colourful piñata are also made as part of the preparations for Christmas. They are hollow clay animals, filled with sweets or coins, and hung up as the centrepiece at parties.

At the end of the Christmas celebrations children are blindfolded and have great fun trying to smash open the piñatas with a stick. When the piñata breaks, it showers sweets and coins all over the party guests.

This colourful Mexican market stall is full of little painted figures that people can buy for their Nativity scene. ▽

Making a Christmas Piñata

1 Tear up old newspaper into strips and glue them over the blown up balloon, using the PVA glue. ▽

You will need:
* Newspaper
* Diluted PVA glue
* Blown up balloon
* Powder paint and brush
* Christmas decorations: tinsel, streamers, ribbons
* Chocolate coins
* Stick and blindfold

4 Put the chocolate coins inside and fill the hole with some crumpled paper. Hang up the piñata at your party and have fun trying to break it open! ▽

2 Cover the balloon completely with about three layers of glued newspaper, and leave to dry. △

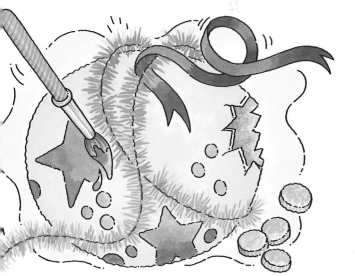

3 Pop the balloon with a pin. Then decorate your piñata. Paint patterns with the powder paint and glue on the tinsel and ribbons. △

Christmas Trees

△ *A large house in Washington, USA is beautifully decorated for Christmas with lights, garlands and wreaths.*

Christmas is one of the most important festivals of the Christian year. Streets and houses are decorated with coloured lights and Christmas trees. It is a time of great joy and celebration when everyone remembers their family and friends with cards, gifts and parties.

The Christmas tree has presents all round it on Christmas Day. Its history goes back hundreds of years when it was the custom in some countries to bring a fir tree inside and decorate it.

Making a Christmas Table Tree

You will need:
* Scrap card
* Thin green card
* Pencil and scissors
* Paper clips
* Drawing pin
* Needle and thread
* Double-sided tape
* Foil-wrapped chocolate mints

1 Make a template by drawing a tree shape on to scrap card. Cut out the template and use it to make three identical trees from the green card. ▽

2 Fold the trees in half and give the centre fold a good crease. Put them on top of each other and hold in place with paper clips. ▽

4 Then open out the sections and attach the chocolate mints to the card with small pieces of double-sided tape. ▽

3 Make four holes along the centre crease with the drawing pin. Make sure the pin goes through all the trees. Then sew thread through these holes to hold the trees together. △

Twelfth Night

△ *The story of the three kings, Caspar, Melchior and Balthasar visiting baby Jesus is told by these children in their Nativity Play.*

The twelfth night after Christmas is the Christian feast of Epiphany. The three kings visited Jesus in the stable at Bethlehem on that night and gave Him gifts of gold, **frankincense** and **myrrh**.

Giving presents is part of Christmas Day celebrations. Twelfth Night is the last day of the festival. Families take down all the Christmas decorations, tidy up their homes and look forward to the new year ahead.

Making Christmas Boxes and Cards

Here are some ideas for using up all the scraps of Christmas paper that are usually thrown away. Make these colourful Christmas boxes and cards for next year!

You will need:

* Scissors
* PVA glue and brush
* Old cardboard boxes
* Scraps of Christmas gift wrap and old cards
* Coloured card

3 Completely cover the box and lid with pictures, and protect the decorated box with a varnish made from PVA mixed with water. ▽

1 Collect up all the scraps of wrapping paper, labels and old cards that are no longer wanted and cut out all the Christmas pictures. △

4 Make labels and cards by using the cut out pictures and gluing them to folded rectangles of coloured card. ▽

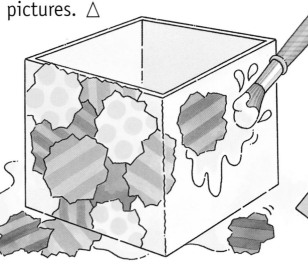

2 Choose a box to cover. Using PVA, glue the pictures to the box. Start on one side, overlapping the pictures so the card does not show. △

Winter Stories

Winter in the **Arctic** is very long and harsh. Days are short, as it gets dark in the early afternoon. For the people that live in these regions, the long dark winter nights are a time for telling stories.

Many years ago the **Inuit** women used to tell stories and legends with little finger puppets, which brought the stories to life. Their legends were often about the creatures and spirits of their lands. They told stories about the moon and stars, and the animals of the Arctic, the seal, walrus, whale and **caribou**.

This Saami (Lapp) family live in a traditional tent in northern Norway, but today most families live in modern houses with central heating. ▽

Making Finger Puppets

You will need:
* Coloured card
* Pair of compasses
* Pencil and ruler
* Scissors
* Glue stick
* Sticky tape
* Large ring pulls

1 Draw circles which measure 10 cm across on to coloured card and cut them out. △

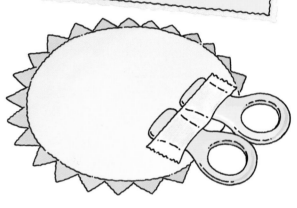

3 Tape two ring pulls to each card face to put your fingers through. △

Make a whole range of animal faces and figures. Then tell a story about them and bring them to life with your fingers.

2 Cut out pieces of coloured paper and glue them to the circles. Make them into faces or figures. △

New Year's Day

△ *A bronze Roman coin shows the two faces of the god Janus, looking back to the past and forward to the future.*

Many people celebrate New Year's Day on 1 January. Others use a different calendar. Some people use the **lunar** calendar which is based on cycles of the moon. The dates of festivals change from year to year.

Julius Caesar started the **Gregorian** calendar. January is named after the Roman god Janus. He had two faces. One looked back on the old year, the other looked forward to the new one. 1 January was a public holiday in Ancient Rome, and it still is today. At midnight on New Year's Eve people celebrate by ringing church bells to welcome in the New Year.

Making A Star Mobile

1 Using the method shown on page 13, draw a large star on to the card and cut it out. ▽

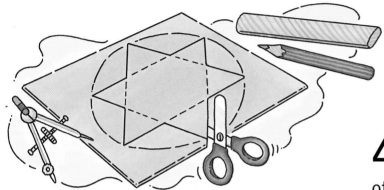

2 Draw smaller circle and star shapes on the coloured card using the compasses. Then cut them all out. ▽

4 Use the hole punch to make holes in the large star and the other shapes. Then tie the shapes to the star with different lengths of string. Try threading several stars to one length of string. Then hang your star mobile up. ▽

3 Decorate some of the circles with scraps of card to make the sun and planets. ▽

Yuan Tan

△ *Chinese New Year is celebrated all over the world, with colourful embroidered costumes and flags, like this parade in Los Angeles.*

Chinese New Year is the most important Chinese festival and lasts for fifteen days. All Chinese birthdays are held at this time, so there is special food, family parties, street parades and fireworks. Children are given presents of 'lucky money' in red and gold envelopes.

Each year is named after twelve animals – the rat, buffalo, tiger, hare, dragon, snake, horse, ram, monkey, rooster, dog and pig. They all have a character – the tiger is brave and the dog is loyal. People who are born in the year of a particular animal are said to be like them.

Making a Chinese Birthday Card

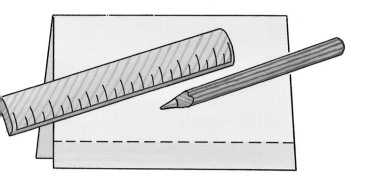

You will need:
* Rectangle of card
* Scissors
* Pencil
* Ruler
* Glue stick
* Coloured card scraps

1 Fold a rectangle of card in half. Draw a dotted line along each side of the card, 1 cm from the edge. △

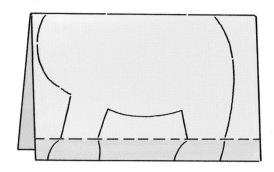

2 Draw a simple animal shape on the folded card. Choose one of the Chinese birthday animals, like the tiger. Make sure the paws are drawn below the dotted line. △

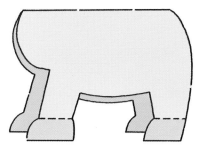

3 Cut out the animal, making sure you cut through both sides of the card. Do not cut along the top fold. △

4 Decorate the animal with scraps of paper. Glue on a face, ears and a tail. △

5 Fold the paws out to make the animal card stand up. Open it out to write any message inside. ▽

Teng Chien

This is the Chinese Lantern festival and takes place on the fifteenth and final day of the Chinese New Year. Animal-shaped lanterns are carried through the streets, the lights symbolize the coming of spring.

The Dance of the Dragon is the most important part of the festival, when huge dragons, symbols of good luck, dance through the streets. The dragon costumes are made from bamboo and coloured silk. They can be up to 30 metres long and need many dancers inside to carry them.

A huge Chinese dragon dances through the streets of Singapore, with great excitement and lots of fireworks. ▽

Making a Dancing Dragon Mask

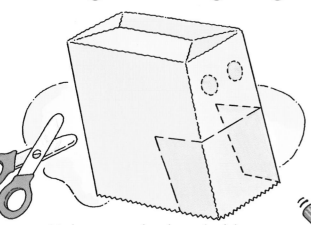

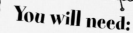

1 Make sure the bag is big enough to go over your head. Cut out a section from the front to make the dragon's snout and holes for the nostrils. △

2 Paint the bag to cover up any printing. When the paint has dried, decorate the bag with shapes cut from the coloured paper. Cut out ears, teeth and scales and glue them to the mask with the glue stick. △

3 Using the sharp pencil point, carefully make a hole in each ping pong ball and also in each side of the bag. Thread one end of the tag through the hole in the ball and the other through the bag to make the dragon's eyes. △

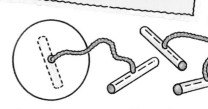

4 Roll strips of coloured paper around the pencil to make the dragon's mane, and attach the strips to the head with sticky tape. Now the dragon is ready to dance! △

Winter Calendar

This calendar refers only to events and festivals mentioned in this book.

Thanksgiving Day
Fourth Thursday in November
First Day of Advent
1 December
St. Nicholas' Day
6 December
Hanukkah (The Jewish Festival of Lights)
Celebrated for 8 days in December
Christmas Day
25 December
New Year's Day
1 January
Twelfth Night
6 January
Yuan Tan (The Chinese New Year)
Celebrated for 15 days in January
Teng Chien (The Chinese Lantern Festival)
Last Day of Yuan Tan

Many religions and cultures use the lunar calendar, which mean that their festivals are not held on the same day every year.

Glossary

ancestors Relatives that lived many years ago.

Arctic The polar region, near the North Pole.

bishop A high priest in the Christian Church.

caribou A herd of reindeer.

circumference The measurement around a circle or sphere.

frankincense A special type of incense.

Gregorian The calendar that usually has 365 days in a year.

hanukia A Jewish candlestick, with nine branches, also called a menorah.

Inuit People who live in the Arctic regions.

lunar Controlled by the moon.

miracle When something unbelievable and wonderful happens.

myrrh A sweet-smelling gum, used to make incense.

native A person who comes from a particular country.

saviour A person who saves the lives of other people.

symbolic When something has a special meaning.

Syrian People who come from Syria, a country in the Middle East.

Books to Read

Information Series

Blueprints *series* (Stanley Thornes) especially *Seasonal Topics* and *Festivals*
My Belief *series* (Franklin Watts)
Our Culture *series* (Franklin Watts)
World-wide Crafts *series* (A & C Black) especially *Celebrations* by Chris Deshpande

Craft series, including Seasons

First Arts and Crafts *series* (Wayland)
Go, Set, Go! *series* (Franklin Watts)
Seasonal Projects *series* (Wayland)
Starting Points *series* (Franklin Watts)

For festival poster: The Festival Shop, 56 Poplar Road, King's Heath, Birmingham B14 7AG.

Index